GECKOS

by Katie Marsico

Children's Press®

An Imprint of Scholastic Inc.
New York Toronto London Auckland Sydney
Mexico City New Delhi Hong Kong
Danbury, Connecticut

Content Consultant
Dr. Stephen S. Ditchkoff
Professor of Wildlife Sciences
Auburn University
Auburn, Alabama

Photographs © 2014: age fotostock: 39 (Environmental Images), cover
(Kitchin & Hurst); Alamy Images/Kathy Hancock: 4, 20; AP Images/
Francois Mori: 40; Dreamstime: 3 foreground, 11 (Swisshippo), 2
background, 3 background, 44 background, 45 background; Getty
Images: 5 top, 15 (Martin Harvey), 5 bottom, 35 (Michael Leach);
Science Source: 7 (Alan & Sandy Carey), 24 (ANT Photo Library), 19
(Chris Mattison/FLPA), 12 (Eye of Science), 16 (Fletcher & Baylis), 23
(Greg Dimijian), 36 (Michael McCoy), 8 (Stuart Wilson), 31 (Volker
Steger); Shutterstock, Inc./Ricardo A. Alves: 28; Superstock, Inc./
Animals Animals: 1, 27, 46; USGS/Robert Fisher: 32.

Library of Congress Cataloging-in-Publication Data
Marsico, Katie, 1980–
  Geckos/By Katie Marsico.
   p. cm.–(Nature's children)
  Summary: "This book details the life and habits of geckos"–
Provided by publisher.
  Audience: 009-012.
  Audience: Grades 4 to 6.
  Includes bibliographical references and index.
  ISBN 978-0-531-23357-3 (lib. bdg.) —
  ISBN 978-0-531-25155-3 (pbk.)
  1. Geckos–Juvenile literature. I. Title. II. Series: Nature's children
(New York, N.Y.)
  QL666.L245M374 2013
  597.95'2–dc23   2013000090

All rights reserved. Published in 2014 by Children's Press, an imprint
of Scholastic Inc.

Printed in China 62
SCHOLASTIC, CHILDREN'S PRESS, and associated logos are
trademarks and/or registered trademarks of Scholastic Inc.

5 6 7 8 9 10 R 23 22 21 20 19 18 17 16

Geckos

Class	Reptilia
Order	Squamata
Family	Gekkonidae
Genera	About 52
Species	Roughly 917
World distribution	Both tropical and temperate climates on every continent except Antarctica
Habitats	Grasslands, mountain ranges, deserts, and rain forests
Distinctive physical characteristics	Flattened body with a short neck, wide head, and thick tail; four feet with five toes on each; scales that feature a variety of colors and patterns; skin coloring can change to blend in with the surrounding environment; tissue around the hind quarters makes it easy for the tail to detach
Habits	Are able to shed skin and tail to escape predators; males are frequently territorial; females generally lay between one and two eggs once or twice a year; do not remain close to care for unborn young
Diet	Different species feed on a variety of foods, including insects, worms, smaller lizards and mammals, moss, flower nectar, and rotting fruit; hatchlings eat smaller insects such as fruit flies

GECKOS

Contents

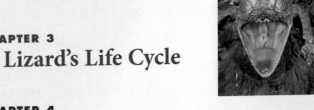

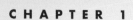

CHAPTER 1

Making Noises in the Moonlight

Night settles over a rain forest in northeastern India. Yet not every creature is asleep within this darkened tropical world. A series of barking and chirping noises echo among the trees. At first, it might seem as if frogs and birds are responsible for the racket. But they are not the only ones creating the haunting chorus that fills the evening air. Geckos are barking and chirping to communicate with one another under the moonlight that sparkles across the lush, green forest.

Geckos are small- to medium-size lizards that are known for their unique vocal abilities and amazing feet. Many of these reptiles actually have adhesive paw pads that allow them to climb smooth surfaces. Scientists recognize roughly 917 species of gecko. They are generally found in warmer temperate and tropical climates all across the globe. The only continent where they do not exist is Antarctica.

The leopard gecko is one of several gecko species found in India.

A Look at the Lizards' Habitats

Several species of gecko are found in rain forests. But this is not the only habitat where these lizards live. Geckos also exist in deserts, mountain ranges, and grasslands.

Some species are terrestrial. This means that they live on the ground. Others are arboreal. These species spend most of their time in trees.

Geckos do best in environments that feature warmer temperatures. This is because they, like all reptiles, are cold-blooded. Their body temperature is affected by the temperature outside. If a particular environment is too cold, a gecko's temperature drops. Its body begins to slow down, and the lizard begins to hibernate.

Wild geckos do not just live outside, though. It is not unusual for these reptiles to make their way inside people's houses. Luckily, a lot of human beings do not view geckos as pests. Because they eat bugs, these lizards are sometimes seen as a natural solution to homeowners' insect problems.

The western banded gecko lives in the deserts of the southwestern United States and northwestern Mexico.

Shapes and Sizes

The smallest gecko is shorter than a grown-up's pinky nail! Dwarf geckos measure just 0.6 inches (1.5 centimeters) long. These tiny reptiles weigh only 1.9 grains (123 milligrams). Meanwhile the world's largest gecko is the New Caledonian giant gecko. This lizard can stretch up to 17 inches (43 cm) from head to tail and can weigh more than 1 pound (0.5 kilograms).

A gecko's flattened body has a short neck, a wide head, and a thick tail. These reptiles have four feet with five toes on each foot. Geckos are covered in scales that come in a wide variety of colors and patterns. Most are tan or gray, while others are bright blue, green, white, orange, or yellow.

Some geckos have spots or stripes. Such designs help geckos blend into their environment. This allows them to avoid predators and to sneak up on prey. Certain species such as the Mediterranean gecko even change color depending on whether it is light or dark outside.

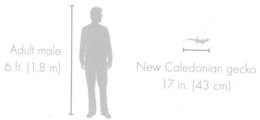

Adult male
6 ft. (1.8 m)

New Caledonian gecko
17 in. (43 cm)

A green gecko's back is sometimes more brightly colored than its belly.

CHAPTER 2

Incredible Adaptations

Geckos' feet are an example of the amazing adaptations that help them survive in the wild. Most gecko species can run up smooth, vertical surfaces with ease. Many animals would find this type of movement challenging. Geckos can do this because they have millions of tiny hairs called setae on the bottoms of their feet. The setae are split into hundreds of tips known as septulae. Together, the setae and septulae create a grip. The result is that geckos' feet have a built-in adhesive that allows the reptiles to cling to whatever surface they are walking across.

Even smooth surfaces such as glass have incredibly tiny bumps and dents. Septulae are so small that they can grip these invisible bumps on a surface.

Scientists use powerful microscopes to get extremely close looks at setae.

Unique Noises and Mighty Mouths

Geckos also possess an important adaptation in their throats. This is where two folds of tissue called vocal cords are located. A gecko's vocal cords vibrate when air passes over them. The vibration creates noises such as chirps, barks, clicks, squeaks, and croaks.

Geckos are the only lizards that have vocal cords. They rely on these tissues to produce a variety of sounds that attract mates and help spread other social messages. Certain calls even manage to scare away enemies.

Depending on the species, a gecko might also use its teeth to keep predators at a distance. Most geckos have roughly 100 teeth at birth. They replace their teeth every few months. Not all geckos are able to deliver a painful bite to defend themselves against enemies. Some do have powerful bites. For example, the tokay gecko has been known to draw blood when its teeth pierce human flesh.

Geckos open their mouths wide to communicate and threaten predators.

Skin That Sheds and a Tear-Apart Tail

A process known as shedding is another example of an adaptation that geckos depend on to stay healthy—and sometimes to escape predators! As they grow, geckos shed their skin to reveal a new coat of scales. Yet some species also shed when they are trapped by an enemy. The old layer of skin peels off while they flee whatever animal is trying to capture them.

Geckos are able to lose their tails for similar reasons. The tissue around a gecko's hindquarters is designed in a way that makes it easy for the tail to break apart from the body. A gecko's tail often continues to wriggle even after it is no longer attached. This frequently distracts predators and gives the lizard an opportunity to run to safety. Luckily, a gecko that loses a tail does not have to live without one forever. It is usually able to grow a replacement in a few months.

Geckos shed their tails by flexing their muscles in a certain way.

Amazing Eyes and Ears

Geckos use their powerful senses to detect danger and track down prey. Scientists say that geckos have remarkable vision. Certain species are among a limited number of animals that are able to see colors at night. In fact, experts estimate that the vision of the helmet gecko is 350 times more sensitive to various colors than human vision!

Most geckos do not have movable eyelids to protect their eyes. Instead, they have a transparent piece of tissue covering each eyeball. They use their tongue to lick this tissue clean.

Scientists believe that geckos also have a strong sense of hearing. Like all reptiles, they lack outer ears. Small holes on either side of their head pick up sound vibrations that then travel to their inner ears.

A gecko's enormous eyes provide it with an extraordinary sense of vision.

A Few Facts About Feeding

Geckos rely on their senses not only to escape predators but also to track down their next meal. Depending on the species, this might be a cricket, beetle, cockroach, or worm. Some geckos eat young scorpions, and small lizards and mammals, too. They have also been known to feed on moss, flower nectar, and rotting fruit.

Wild geckos spend much of their time searching for food. They often stalk prey and then lunge forward when it is within reach. Certain geckos even use their jaws to swing their victims against the ground. This technique helps stun larger prey and makes it easier to overpower them.

Geckos have special adaptations that prevent them from starving when they become less active during cooler weather. When the temperature drops, their metabolism slows down. During this time, many geckos live off fat stored in other parts of their body, including their tails.

Insects and spiders make tasty treats for most gecko species.

CHAPTER 3

A Lizard's Life Cycle

Most geckos are solitary animals. This means that they prefer to live alone. In fact, it is not unusual for male geckos to be quite territorial. They make noises such as clicks and chirps to warn other animals to keep away from areas where they feed and mate.

These types of sounds are only one way that geckos communicate. Body language is another. Geckos often use tail movements to send signals that give clues about what they are feeling. For example, they tend to swish their tails slowly if they are threatened. Scientists have observed that a male moves the tip of his tail more quickly when he is interested in mating with a female.

In most cases, geckos generally come together only to produce young. But not all geckos have to do this. Some are able to have babies even without mating! Certain species such as the mourning gecko are capable of asexual reproduction.

Geckos generally spend most of their time alone except during mating season.

From Eggs to Little Lizards

After mating, female geckos usually lay eggs. A few species in New Zealand give birth to live young, however. Depending on the species, geckos generally lay anywhere from one to several clutches per year. The number of eggs per clutch varies for each species.

Females tend to lay eggs under rocks, leaves, or tree bark. Some species produce eggs that are soft and leathery. Other geckos lay eggs that feature a harder shell.

In either case, females do not stick around to care for their unborn young. It takes several weeks for the eggs to hatch. The baby geckos, or hatchlings, are able to survive on their own from the moment they poke through their shell. At first, they mainly feed on whatever prey they can easily catch, including small insects such as fruit flies.

FUN FACT! The temperature of the nest helps determine the gender of gecko hatchlings. Warmer temperatures usually result in a larger number of male lizards.

Female Madagascar giant day geckos usually lay two eggs at a time.

Everyday Activities and Behavior

It does not take long for young geckos to reach adulthood. These lizards are typically ready to mate when they are between one and two years old. In the meantime, they learn how to track down prey, avoid predators, and locate mates. Geckos can live up to 20 years in the wild.

Most geckos are nocturnal. This means that they are more active at night than during the day. Nocturnal geckos hunt and mate in darkness. They rest in trees, on rocks, or in burrows when it is light outside. The opposite is true for various species of day geckos. These reptiles are diurnal, which means they are awake during the day. They tend to search for prey and mates from late morning until midafternoon.

Geckos have different hibernation patterns depending on where they live. Species in tropical areas rarely hibernate. This is because temperatures there remain warm all year. Geckos in temperate climates slow down during cooler seasons. They hibernate in underground holes and small cracks in rocks.

The leopard gecko is among the many nocturnal gecko species.

CHAPTER 4

Prehistory to the Present

Geckos have had quite a while to adapt to the world around them. The earliest reptiles walked the earth roughly 315 million years ago.

The earliest-known gecko fossil dates back about 100 million years. Experts say these remains show that geckos had setae on their feet even then. They think that this unique adaptation has changed a great deal throughout history. Scientists say it is likely that different groups of geckos gained and lost their sticky toe pads over time.

The development of setae appears to be linked to changes in the prehistoric lizards' environments. Geckos that once existed in areas with lots of boulders and trees tended to have setae more often than geckos living on the ground or on sandy surfaces. In other words, their famous toe pads seem to have developed in settings where they were most needed for easy movement.

Many modern gecko species rely heavily on their sticky feet.

Lizards Like Leopards and Bees

The roughly 917 species of gecko that exist today each have amazing and sometimes mysterious traits that scientists are eager to learn more about. Many people are familiar with leopard geckos because they are often kept as pets. In the wild, this species can be found in the rocky deserts and scrubs of south-central Asia. Leopard geckos got their name because—like actual leopards—they are yellow or white with dark brown spots. These lizards are different from several other species of gecko because they possess movable eyelids. In addition, they lack adhesive toe pads.

The bumblebee gecko also has no adhesive toe pads. This species was recently discovered by scientists in the rain forests of Papua New Guinea north of Australia. A series of gold and black bands was what led people to name these geckos after the similarly colored bumblebee. Experts believe that bumblebee geckos rely on their stripes to blend in with the rain forest floor.

The bumblebee gecko grows to be about 5 inches (13 centimeters) long.

Webbing and Waterproof Scales

Interesting coloring is just one example of what makes certain species of gecko unique. For instance, the Namib Desert gecko is known for its webbed feet. It relies on this adaptation to scurry across and dig burrows in the hot sand of southwestern Africa.

Flying geckos—also called parachute geckos—have webbing as well. Of course, they do not actually fly. Extra flaps of skin around the head, body, legs, and tail simply provide them with added lift as they leap across tree branches in Southeast Asia.

Some geckos have certain physical features that help them avoid drowning. The Brazilian pygmy gecko is so tiny that a raindrop would wash over it like a tidal wave and drown it if it weren't for its waterproof skin. Its scales do not absorb, or take in, moisture. As a result, Brazilian pygmy geckos are able to survive even the deadliest of raindrops!

FUN FACT! A gecko depends on its tail to help balance the weight of its body as it speeds across a surface.

The webbed skin on flying geckos help them make spectacular leaps.

A Peek at Pygopods

One of the gecko's most remarkable relatives is the pygopod. At first, these reptiles—often called legless or flap-footed lizards—might not seem to have much in common with geckos. Pygopods actually look a lot more like snakes than lizards. They have long, thin bodies and are either completely missing limbs or have small flaps where their legs would usually be. The 41 species of pygopod are native to Australia and Papua New Guinea.

Geckos and pygopods share a few important traits. For starters, both feature species that do not possess movable eyelids. Like most geckos, pygopods also generally only lay a few eggs in each clutch. Finally, both reptiles are unique because they are able to use vocalization to create noises. Pygopods are known for their ability to produce barks and squeaks.

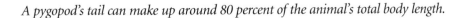

A pygopod's tail can make up around 80 percent of the animal's total body length.

CHAPTER 5

Increasing Human Awareness

Geckos are amazing animals, but they face an uncertain future. Many human activities have led certain species to be listed as endangered or threatened. This means that they are either at immediate risk of being completely wiped off the planet or likely to face such a risk in the near future.

One of the major threats that many geckos face is destruction of their natural habitat. People continue to clear forests and grasslands to develop farms, roads, towns, and cities. As they do, geckos and countless other animals lose habitats that they rely on to feed and reproduce. Pollution also has a harmful effect on such environments. Chemicals ruin the water, air, and soil that numerous creatures—including geckos—depend on to survive.

The clearing of rain forests leaves geckos with fewer places to live.

Other Threats and Long-Term Answers

The exotic pet trade is another activity that places various species of gecko at risk. Many of these lizards make excellent pets and are captured to be sold in pet stores. This practice does not always have a destructive impact on geckos. However, it sometimes causes problems in areas where wild populations are already suffering from other threats. In addition, some people hunt and kill geckos so that they can use their body parts to prepare traditional medicines.

Scientists are discovering new information about geckos every day. They are even learning about species that they never realized existed in the past. Yet conservationists understand that they need to make an effort if they want to continue studying geckos in the future. They are working to educate the public about these remarkable lizards and the dangers they face. They are raising awareness that geckos are unique and exciting animals that deserve protection and respect.

Scientists continue to discover new gecko species and learn more about these incredible lizards.

Words to Know

adaptations (ad-ap-TAY-shuhnz) — changes in animals or plants so that they better fit a new setting or set of circumstances

adhesive (ad-HEE-siv) — able to stick to a surface or object

asexual (ay-SEK-shoo-uhl) — reproduction that does not involve mating

clutches (KLUHCH-iz) — nests of eggs

conservationists (kon-sur-VAY-shun-ists) — people who work to protect an environment and the living things in it

environments (en-VYE-ruhn-muhnts) — the natural surroundings of living things, such as the air, land, or sea

fossil (FAH-suhl) — a bone, shell, or other trace of an animal or plant from long ago, preserved as rock

habitat (HAB-uh-tat) — the place where an animal or a plant is usually found

hibernate (HYE-bur-nate) — to pass the entire winter sleeping or resting; hibernation protects animals and helps them survive when temperatures are cold and food is hard to find

mates (MAYTZ) — animals that join together to reproduce

metabolism (muh-TAB-uh-liz-uhm) — the rate at which an animal uses energy

native (NAY-tiv) — naturally belonging to a certain place

pollution (puh-LOO-shuhn) — harmful materials that damage or contaminate the air, water, and soil

predators (PRED-uh-turz) — animals that live by hunting other animals for food

prey (PRAY) — an animal that's hunted by other animals for food

reptiles (REP-tilez) — cold-blooded animals that crawl across the ground or creep on short legs; most reptiles have backbones and reproduce by laying eggs

scrubs (SKRUHBZ) — low bushes or short trees that grow close together and cover an area of land

species (SPEE-sheez) — one of the groups into which animals and plants of the same genus are divided; members of the same species can mate and have offspring

temperate (TEM-pur-ut) — having a temperature that is rarely very high or very low, such as a temperate climate

territorial (ter-uh-TOR-ee-uhl) — defensive of a certain area

transparent (trans-PAIR-uhnt) — clear like glass, allowing light through so that objects on the other side can be seen clearly

Habitat Map

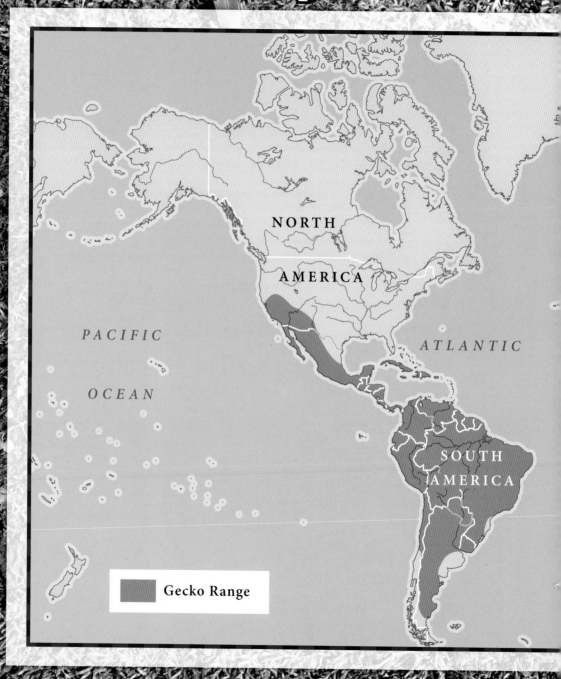

NORTH AMERICA

PACIFIC OCEAN

ATLANTIC

SOUTH AMERICA

Gecko Range

ARCTIC OCEAN

ASIA

EUROPE

PACIFIC OCEAN

AFRICA

INDIAN OCEAN

OCEAN

AUSTRALIA

Find Out More

Books

Bartlett, R. D., and Patricia Bartlett. *Leopard and Fat-Tailed Geckos*. Hauppauge, NY: Barron's, 2009.

Bredeson, Carmen. *Flying Geckos and Other Weird Reptiles*. Berkeley Heights, NJ: Enslow, 2010.

Connors, Kathleen. *Geckos*. New York: Gareth Stevens, 2013.

Visit this Scholastic Web site for more information on geckos:
www.factsfornow.scholastic.com
Enter the keyword **Geckos**

Index

Page numbers in *italics* indicate a photograph or map.

(Index continued)

About the Author

Katie Marsico is the author of more than 100 children's books. She never knew about geckos' fun feet or cool vocal abilities before writing this book. She dedicates this work to her daughter's school, Edison Elementary in Elmhurst, Illinois.